About the Author

A native of Tennessee, single, and loving myself accordingly. I'm a forty-eight year-old vegan nature lover who's extremely addicted to books, lifting weights, taking naps, and inspiring others to embrace the perspectives of others.

Single By Choice

Wanna L Cunningham

Single By Choice

Olympia Publishers
London

www.olympiapublishers.com
OLYMPIA PAPERBACK EDITION

Copyright © Wanna L Cunningham 2024

The right of Wanna L Cunningham to be identified as author of this work has been asserted in accordance with sections 77 and 78 of the Copyright, Designs and Patents Act 1988.

All Rights Reserved

No reproduction, copy or transmission of this publication
may be made without written permission.
No paragraph of this publication may be reproduced,
copied or transmitted save with the written permission of the publisher,
or in accordance with the provisions
of the Copyright Act 1956 (as amended).

Any person who commits any unauthorised act in relation to
this publication may be liable to criminal
prosecution and civil claims for damage.

A CIP catalogue record for this title is
available from the British Library.

ISBN: 978-1-80074-824-8

This is a work of fiction.
Names, characters, places and incidents originate from the writer's imagination. Any resemblance to actual persons, living or dead, is purely coincidental.

First Published in 2024

Olympia Publishers
Tallis House
2 Tallis Street
London
EC4Y 0AB

Printed in Great Britain

Dedication

To my angel, Grace.

Acknowledgements

A special thanks to everyone who inspired and encouraged me to share my message with the world.

First, I'd like to start off by saying that I am not a relationship expert. I'm not a counselor, nor am I a psychologist. Honestly, I like to call myself a "life experience learner", and what I mean by that is I actually enjoy both the ups and downs that come with relationships and their endings, but I particularly LOVE to analyze the lessons that occur throughout the entire relationship process. To me, this is the area that most people neglect to reflect upon after a break-up. This is a failure of great proportion because the lessons are where we find out who we truly are, and what it is we desire in a potential mate. Over the course of my life, I've been married and single, looking for love and not looking, or not caring. One of the keys to being in a meaningful relationship is genuinely being able to relate to the other person involved. Even more important is the internal happiness that you possess before you present yourself as "available". It takes a lot to admit that you are not happy or fulfilled, so we sometimes use that inability as a way to search for that certain something, or someone, to fill that void. The truth is that nothing ever REALLY fills that void and the love that you seek already resides within you. This may be hard to recognize, especially when we don't take the time to breathe after a relationship is over. Though sometimes painful, the "end" is our opportunity to get back to the beginning of ourselves, and what we need in order to heal. I've learned the lessons; I listen to my gut and that little voice in my head regarding love. There are obstacles, and there are obstacle courses, and I've learned that the courses are way more exhausting. This book is intended to be an inspiration for those who have decided, like me, to drop out of the race.

Not indefinitely, but for however long is needed. It has been six years and counting on my end, and it has all been by choice. I cannot tell you how long you have to remain by yourself, but that is just the point. It is all up to you. I, personally, have no desire to settle for something that is not conducive to my happiness.

After spending seventeen years in a marriage which no longer exists, I feel that I have earned the right to accept or reject that which is best for me. That is the benefit of being in love with yourself and knowing your worth. There is nothing wrong with you. You are not self-absorbed or self-centered. You are simply taking this time to learn from the lessons. I hope that my advice can help you along the way.

Chapter One

Single by Choice... What is This?

It is important to note that you are not obligated to be in a relationship. Although we are led to believe that there is a timeframe for us to achieve certain goals, you know, the belief that we should be married by the age of twenty-five, settled by the age of thirty, and having kids by a particular age, there is no timeframe. You create your own reality, and the choices you make help to develop that reality. This book is not intended to bash men or to create some feminist movement. It is simply words expressing the importance of knowing your self-worth, and what it is you deserve. There are so many definitions of what it means to be single; you have those who are single and not happy about it, those who are single and actively looking, those who are single because they are waiting and taking the steps to better improve themselves before entering a relationship, and you have those who are currently single and happy and not seeking anything except the knowledge of who they truly are. This is what I mean when I say single by choice. There is this misconception that you cannot be single and happy, or that you cannot be single and live a successful and fruitful life. It is not one particular person's fault that we think this way. Most of us were raised to accept this ideology as the best; you finish school and you go back to school, and you marry and have children, and you get a home, and you live to be eighty years old, sitting on the porch in a rocking chair, sipping lemonade, and then you die. Some find that whole thought process to be totally archaic. They choose not to settle for tradition, and they carve their own paths. They take their time on their journey. This is not to speak against anyone who believes in traditional thinking. After all, it IS traditional thinking, and we bind ourselves to traditions and our cultural and religious beliefs. That is just a part of who we are; it is part of our DNA and the fabric of what makes us who we are. That is not to say that we don't have the right to rewrite our own stories. So, single by choice... what is it? It is simply an individual who decides to wait for a relationship to naturally occur. There is no rushing. There is no speed dating. There is no bar-hopping, no one-night stands. There is just a person who is waiting to find what it is they truly want, and something that makes them happier than what they already are. When you are not worried about relationships or how you're going to meet the next person in your life, you rid yourself of excess stress. Most people who are stress-free are happy. They do not count the hours that go by; they don't stare at the clock or cry in the corner. They simply accept the way that life has been dealt to them regarding relationships, and they are fine with it. They are not ready to take that next step, and they understand that there is absolutely nothing wrong with taking their time. They understand that being in a relationship is not something that they have to do. It is not a prerequisite for living a good life. Even though the opposite has been drilled into our heads a million times by Harlequin novels and romantic comedies, they recognize that those are all bodies of fiction. People who wait value themselves, and they value the whole concept of being in a relationship. It is not something to be rushed into, especially when you are in the process of learning the lessons from previous relationships. You take those mistakes which were made by yourself and your previous partner, and you try to avoid making those same mistakes over and over again. You may be called anti-social, snobby, out of touch with reality, and a party pooper. This is definitely not the case, and you should not be made to feel this way. You're simply taking control of your own life and getting in front of your own decisions; being in control of your own decision making and understanding that the process of being in a relationship takes more than just saying, "I have a girlfriend/boyfriend." So, you choose to wait. No big deal. This is an opportunity for you to get to know who you truly are; what you want, what you desire. You should already be engulfed in self-happiness by the time you reach this point. So, you're looking for someone who is just as happy as you are. By happy, I mean whole and complete, with an understanding of who they are inside. Your happiness is not hinged upon what another person does and vice versa. The two of you are willing to make the same sacrifice, and that sacrifice is being able to stand before each other and say, "I am truly ready for commitment. I am truly ready to be truthful and honest. I am truly ready to give you my complete and total self. And I am ready to be a counterpart in a happy union with you." This all sounds well and fine because this is how a relationship should truly be. But until we have found that counterpart, and we have found in another person what we see in ourselves; what we are able to reflect in ourselves, we are not in that big of a hurry. We go out to eat. We go to the movies. We travel the world. We shop. We do everything that single, actively-looking people do. I have, myself, been looked at like a science project, and have had people try to dissect who I am because I'm not part of the norm; I don't fit inside the box.

But as I have become more accustomed to the idea of being single by choice, I have grown to be less offended by it. Being single does not mean that you are cursed. Being single does not mean that nobody wants you. It also doesn't mean that you are denying yourself the chance of being with someone. It only means that you refuse to settle for something less than what you know you want, and something less than what you know you deserve. And so, you go on throughout your day, observing and learning and listening to relationship problems, and you are grateful and thankful that you do not have to deal with them.

That is a good thing. No one wants to be in an unhappy relationship, or a relationship that they feel "obligated" to stay in; good or bad. The obligation is not there when you are single, and even less when you are choosing to be single. You make your own decisions regarding who you want to share your time with. This could ultimately be the individual you end up spending the rest of your life with. Why would you not want to make the absolute best choice when it comes to what you need?

Chapter Two

Sitting in the Hurt

We all know, pretty much, how the story goes. Boy meets girl, they date for an extended period of time, they fall in love, they have their problems, their ups and downs, boy leaves girl, or girl leaves boy, and then they both jump back into relationships without so much as taking a breath. This is how relationships usually happen. They start off fresh like flowers, and then like flowers, they wither and die. I don't mean to sound harsh, but it is a harsh reality. Not giving yourself a chance to breathe or reflect upon what just took place after a relationship is over, is one of the worst ways to begin to heal. The best part about the entire situation is that you have this chance to gather up the crumbs after the cookies crumble, and try to piece yourself back together again.

    One thing that we all have a tendency to do is to move on immediately, not knowing that we are setting ourselves up to return back to a relationship that is very much similar to the one we walked away from. This is why it's so important for us to sit in the hurt. We have to sit in the hurt. We have to feel the pain. We have to feel the numbness that comes with heartache. There are some relationships that you can slap a bandage on, and there are some that are beyond repair. Regardless of the shape, you come out in, it is still an opportunity to regain the pieces of yourself that make you who you are. Heartache is supposed to hurt. It's not supposed to be laughed at. It's not supposed to be a fleeting feeling. It's supposed to be painful and make you look at the entire situation. You try to figure out what happened, and try to keep it from happening again. It does not matter if it is a two-month fling or a ten-year whirlwind romance. The end is always the same. It's the end. It is the end of that relationship. It is the end of that line. As painful as it may seem, it is what you need at that point, otherwise, it would not exist. Have you ever known someone to be in a relationship, and that relationship ends, and then they're in another relationship about a month later, and then THAT relationship ends because of the very same reasons that the previous relationship ended? That happens because the person is not giving themselves time to heal. They are not sitting to themselves and absorbing the pain. They create these barriers or defence mechanisms, and they are put up to keep the pain out. Unbeknownst to them, the pain is exactly what they need. There are also those who do not seem content unless they are in a relationship. It does not matter who the person is, whether or not they are mistreated or disrespected, or even abused. They are just happy with being in a relationship and being able to say it. But in the end, what do they have to show for it? A broken heart? Not being able to accept kindness when it is genuine? Thinking that being mistreated is what they deserve? When you keep putting your mind through the process of being abused and accepting it, even expecting it, you train yourself to look for things that you don't need. That is the reason why some people go from abusive relationship to abusive relationship to abusive relationship; their bodies and minds have adapted to being abused. That is how they think they should be treated, but what they REALLY need to do is take advantage of the opportunity to stop and breathe; take the time to figure out what it is they truly want. This is why sitting in the hurt is so important. You learn when you are hurting. You reflect when you are hurting. You think back on what you should have done when you're hurting. When you ignore the pain and just go on about your daily life as if nothing has happened, you leave yourself open to more of the same. I have never been in a physically abusive relationship, but I have been in a mentally and verbally abusive one. I kept looking for things that were wrong within myself, instead of realizing that the entire relationship was wrong altogether. It was not until I took the time to breathe and be still, that I was able to realize just how unhappy I was. It took that pain, and sitting there, and absorbing it, and soaking it up. It took all of that for me to recognize just how much I didn't want that for myself, and that he was not who I needed to be in a relationship with. That relationship, however, taught me a valuable lesson; I do not have to put up with that. I do not have to put up with being disrespected, with the name-calling, or the manipulation. But you don't know that until you take the time to sit down with yourself and feel the pain and sit in the hurt. You don't realize just how miserable you are. It is so important to look at the lessons. Relationships are all lessons to be learned. If you are with someone who treats you like a princess or a king, you take from that and you keep that to yourself, and you recognize that, should the relationship ever come to an end, you know exactly what you want from your next relationship; you want to be treated as respectfully as you were in that past relationship. You won't accept anything less than that. The lack of wanting to hurt is what keeps you from your bright spot. It is what keeps you from shining your light. No one wants to be hurt. No one wants to feel the pain of a break-up, but, it happens every day. And the best thing that comes from a relationship's ending is the lesson. I stress this so much because this is where you get back to yourself. You pull yourself back up, you pull yourself back together, you look at what you've done, you look at what you went through, you pick apart the good and the bad things, how you felt, you keep the good, and the bad as well, because the bad is your lesson. Never discard your lesson. It is how you learn. I was with the same person for seventeen years, so you can imagine the number of lessons that came from that relationship. That was seventeen years to pick apart from my marriage, the things that I wanted, and the things I didn't want. You have to be honest with yourself.

When you are not happy, you should be able to express your unhappiness. You should not have to shove that down or be made to gloss it over. Pain is pain, and it is supposed to hurt.

You are also supposed to be able to express that. When you don't express that, you carry it over into your next relationship, and it ends up being a different person/the same situation every single time. Relationships are not easy. You go into an "agreement" with a complete stranger, and you try to get to know this stranger as much as you possibly can. The problem is that you will more than likely NOT find out everything you should know until the relationship has long progressed past the stage of holding hands. There are some relationships that last forty, fifty, even sixty years, like my grandparents; sixty-four years, to be exact. I am almost certain that that relationship has had its share of ups and downs, but a union of sixty-four years is one of great resilience; one that most people strive for. There is no doubt that relationship dynamics have changed since the days my grandparents got together. The way we meet people, the way we interact, the way we socialize has all changed.

This also means that our tolerance has changed and that relationships don't last as long as they used to. I'm not saying that you should go into a relationship like you would a bunker, prepared for a natural disaster to strike, but you learn the lessons as you go. You pad yourself, and you protect yourself as you go. You sit in the hurt of those lessons, take mental notes, and keep them there for future use. Relationships are no different from the old adage of "history repeats itself"; if you don't learn, then you are destined to repeat the same mistakes. Feel the pain. Cry. Scream. Punch the pillow. Just feel it. When you allow yourself to feel it, you appreciate it more. That's one more lesson in your belt. That's one more lesson you get to keep for a lifetime. You choose to be single after a relationship has ended; not because you hate men or women, but because you love yourself enough to give yourself the time it takes to heal. You don't want to begin a relationship by pouring your pain onto it. Flowers cannot bloom when they are covered in pain. You are the flower. And you should take care of yourself.

Chapter Three

Where Did Everybody Go?

There is no harm that comes with telling this truth. When you choose to be single, you choose to be alone. As you begin to accept this, you will notice that everybody around you may not understand your new way of thinking. This is understandable. When people have difficulty understanding something, they tend to shy away from it. You should recognize that this does not exclude you. These people could be close friends and family whom you've known your entire life, and you should not blame them for their lack of understanding. After all, you are going against the norm. They may see you as someone who is going through a phase, or someone who's adopting/following the latest trend. It will be entirely up to you to sit down and discuss your choices if that is what you want to do. Of course, you are not obligated to explain yourself when you are doing what's best for you. This also goes for your closest friends whom you may have done some of the wildest things with. They may be more taken aback than your family. They may not understand, or want to accept, your newfound way of living, especially when they are accustomed to calling you up and heading out for a night on the town. This is when you may be looked upon as weird or anti-social, or strange. Try not to take this to heart. People fear what they do not understand, and when they fear something, they tend to walk away.

Being alone may be truly disheartening for you, and the rollercoaster of emotions that come along with it may be entirely new to you. I have had friends who appeared to disown me because I would much rather sit at home than go out socializing to pick up dates. They just could not understand, or get with, what I was going through. Telling someone that you are purposely not looking for a date could lead them to believe that something is wrong with you. It's just not what the average person is used to hearing. As I mentioned before, it became easier for me to not be offended by it. What seems weird to other people is perfectly normal to me, and when people want to walk away, I let them. I know that what I choose to do is totally up to me. You are not alone in this journey, even if there is no one that you know, personally, who is going through this with you. As you grab onto the reins of your new lifestyle choice, you will notice that, as people disappear, new people begin to come into your life. This is because the way you're living now has begun to act like a filter. You know exactly what you want, and who you want to be around, so the universe creates an atmosphere for like-minded people to come through. Although you may not know these people personally, you may meet them through social media and other outlets. You do not have to worry about meeting these people for you will draw them towards you. Other "weird" people will notice you, and you will notice that you have time for new things. Your family may not agree with your ideals but I am almost certain that they will not disown you.

Friends may be a little different, but they do not have to be a part of your life, or as close to you as a family member could be. This may make you sad in the beginning, but as you get better acclimated to your new way of living, choosing to be single, you will start to notice less, and you will stop caring about being accepted. If you are an introvert like myself, you may become more introverted. This is ok. The problem lies, however, with those who are extroverted.

It may be harder for some to accept that you no longer want to do the things you used to do. Think of all the greats throughout history, who had ideas that people neglected to accept, ideas that were thought to come from another planet, but who kept on going. They kept pushing forward. They kept being who they were without dismissing their own personal feelings. You are no different from Einstein... you are no different from Mark Zuckerberg... you are no different from MLK. These individuals all had their own ideas and their own way of doing things that may have seemed strange and may have caused close family and friends to reject them. But, somehow, they persevered. And even though you are not creating a new theory of relativity, you are forging ahead on your own path.

That being said, you may find yourself alone in more ways than one. You should be prepared for this. It may hurt a little, but it is not the end of the world, and you will grow to accept and love your choice. I spend countless hours reading and walking through the park, meditating and nurturing my internal self. I would choose those activities over attending a loud concert or sitting at the end of a bar. There is nothing wrong with doing those things if that is what you choose to do, but when you are choosing to be single, you're choosing to get to know yourself better. A big part of doing that is learning how to embrace solitude. It is where you find yourself. Having a chance to sit and think and reflect, and getting to know who you are is a big part of healing from previous pain. It is a big step toward understanding what it is you truly want. I am, by no means, a religious person. I am, however, an immensely spiritual being beyond anything else. My spirituality is a huge part of who I am, but I would never attempt to convert anyone with my beliefs. This is what works best for me. Knowing who I truly am, and knowing that other people do not define who I am, makes it easier for me to be alone and have a greater understanding of what I want in a potential mate, as well as what I want for myself. I cannot do that in a crowded bar. I can't even do that at family gatherings. Being alone works for me. If you are choosing to be single, if you are choosing to be alone, you are probably not too far removed from my way of thinking. You may seek out that solitude for yourself. The way you choose to socialize and interact with other people may have already changed, and you should not have to apologize for it. Allow your heart to remain open throughout this process, for people will come, and people will go. Regardless of the direction they might take, you will grow to appreciate their honesty. Because you are not taking offense to their reactions, you too will gain a new way of understanding. So, when your ego asks the question, "Where did everybody go", you'll just shrug your shoulders, loving yourself the way you always do.

Chapter Four

Acceptance

Just like any other life-altering experience, choosing to be single will present you with a wide array of challenges. You are intentionally choosing to be alone. Over the course of time, you will come to accept this as normal. You will begin to accept this process as the way you prefer to do things. As I grew more accustomed to the realization or idea of being single on purpose, there was an overwhelming sense of normalcy that I didn't feel I had to change. As mentioned in the previous chapter, you will find yourself physically alone more often than not, but you will begin to appreciate those moments for the blessings that they truly are. Every journey to acceptance will be different. There may be times when you feel like throwing the whole concept away and seriously consider going back to settling for relationships that you don't want, and that are not good for you.

It is very tempting in the beginning. But when you've gone from one relationship to the next, and the next several times over, that alternative seems to just pass away. You are single because you want to be, not because someone is forcing you to or because you have a problem snagging a date. Accepting yourself as single is not a death sentence. It's simply a choice. You have every right to make this choice for yourself. As I mentioned before, you will sometimes be ridiculed for making this choice. At the end of the day, however, that is their opinion, and they are entitled to have one. Accept this time of solitude. Accept this time of getting to know yourself. Accept the fact that you don't have to choose, at this point in time, whether or not you want to be in a relationship. So often, society tries to tell us what we need to do regarding relationships, being single or being alone. We are taught that being single is a miserable way of living; we cannot be happy alone; we grow old and die lonely. This is a concept that we need to get rid of. Being happy has little to do with who you're dating. It does, however, have everything to do with who you are inside. If you are not happy with yourself, you cannot expect to find happiness outside of yourself, nor can you expect someone to come into your life and "do" the work for you. These messages speak against everything in relation to the love of self. Loving yourself is what helps to create this moment of acceptability. I love myself enough to know that I don't have to depend on anyone outside of myself to create happiness for me. I love myself enough to know this to be true. Oftentimes, we are made to believe that if we are alone, we are lacking love, that no one loves us, that we are unlovable. When you accept yourself and your choices as your own, you will immediately begin to notice how you fail to resonate with any of these societal messages. The ideologies that try to connect being single with being sad are, in my opinion, both outdated and outlandish. I know so many people who are in relationships and are miserable. They have also confided in me, speaking of how they secretly wish to be single because they miss their freedom to choose. So do not shy away from this opportunity to accept what is. You chose this, and this is what works for you. There would be times that I'd be strolling through the park or walking around town, and I would see a couple all cuddled and cozied up, holding hands, and I would say to myself, "Ahhh, I wish I had that."

But the truth of the matter is that whomever you choose to be in a relationship with has to want the same things as you do in order for the relationship to work. This goes back to you actually being able to relate to this person. I have nothing against relationships or love; the two go hand in hand and I am very fond of both. I just choose not to settle for anything less than I deserve.

This particular mindset comes partially from those relationship lessons, the ones I chose to pay attention to after they had ended, the ones I most regret. This is when I learned not to settle anymore, and where I learned to accept myself as more important.

When you recognize your worth, it's hard for someone to disrespect you. When you recognize your worth, it's hard for someone to mistreat you. When you recognize your worth, you refuse to settle. Accept yourself as single. Embrace everything that comes with it. This is the way things are for now. Try your best not to fall back into the old habit of just accepting anyone or anything in your life. Another thing you will encounter is the unwillingness of others to accept you as you are. As I mentioned before, not everybody chooses to be single because something happened to them in the past, or because of some previous experience. Some people simply choose to be by themselves. Not everyone will accept you and your new way of thinking. It seems foreign to most people, the idea that you would want to refrain from dating altogether. At the end of the day, you must remember that it is not their choice. This is what you're choosing for yourself and this is what works best for you.

It should not matter to others how you choose to live your personal life, but you will be surprised by how often they voice their opinions, even when you have not asked for them. Go ahead and be single. You are not depriving yourself of anything, despite what others may think. When you accept this part of your life, others should be willing to accept you, as well as your choices. If they don't, then that is their choice as well. Accept yourself for who you are. You're becoming a new person with a new outlook on the things you want out of life. With your newfound acceptance comes an appreciation for the freedom to do as you choose. During my own journey of acceptance, I've become so much more aware of the things I want and the things I deserve. My mind is much clearer than before, and this is why I don't see this journey as a struggle or a challenge as I did in the past. I just see it as what's best for me at this current time.

Hopefully, throughout your journey of acceptance, you will come to find something similar for yourself. It is not hard to abstain from the things that aren't conducive to your happiness and/or progress. It's not difficult. You are who you are at this point in time. You want what you want at this point in time. Choosing to accept this part of who you are is an amazing feat. You should be proud of your choice now, as well as the relationship choices you will make in the future. As time passes, you will begin to notice just how little an issue this has become; you will grow to understand everything that comes with it. You will also notice that it's mostly pressure from others that tends to trigger you, not your own thoughts about the matter. But, just like everything else that doesn't stimulate progression in your life, you will be able to push that away. Know that accepting yourself for who you are is most important. Your commitment to change, your commitment to acceptance, is something to smile at. Your journey has just begun.

Chapter Five

What Temptation?

When I first sat down to peg the title of this chapter, I started laughing because the definition of temptation basically says that there is an urge or desire to do something unwise or unsavory.

As human beings, we are all tempted, at some time or another, to do things that we probably shouldn't do. When you are trying to watch your weight, you are sometimes tempted to eat cookies; when you're on the road to recovery from an addiction, you're sometimes tempted to fall back into old patterns of behaviour. It's important to know, however, that being tempted to do certain things won't cause you to be persecuted; you'll probably just feel bad for a moment after you've committed your crime. But with this chapter, I wanted to speak more on the idea of being tempted to search for ways to satisfy those intimate cravings and random sexual desires. In the beginning stages of my decision to be single, as you could probably imagine, the temptation to go back to the ways of the past was overwhelming.

We seem to have this inherent way of resolving old relationship patterns. They seldom work, especially after we've been intimate with one another. Nevertheless, we are physical beings with desires and expectations of intimacy and some form of human contact or touch. So, the desire to be with someone, the desire to fulfil this need, is hard to resist. We sometimes feel that being physical with someone is a great way to numb ourselves from emotional pain. But as you become more inclined to embrace the single lifestyle that you are presently living, the urge to fulfil these voids with random people starts to wane. Over the course of time, you will begin to learn that intimacy and sex are ways that we exchange energy with one another, and exchanging this energy freely can sometimes lead to an absorption of negativity. You will begin to understand the importance of saving your energy for those who are worthy of it, while simultaneously losing the urgency to "spread" your love like seeds in a garden.

You become more particular about the choices you make when it comes to being physical with someone. We are not robots. We all have a natural desire, at some point, to be with other people. So, when I say what temptation, I'm speaking of how you will, over the course of time, lose these urgencies of randomness; they will cease to exist. You will begin to value your body more. You will not want to give your energy to strangers. You will gain a better understanding of what it means to be intimate, and appreciate the beauty of sharing intimate moments with those who deserve you. Like I said in the beginning, the urges will be there simply because we are men and women who have needs. This is a good time to channel your energy toward other things. Perhaps there are some projects you need to finish or some new venture you wanted to involve yourself in which could get your creative juices flowing.

You may also begin to pick up more hobbies that force

you to become more focused on your inner self and what you need to heal. As you do this, you will gain a better perspective about who you truly are. Moving forward, your desires will eventually subside. They will be there, just not on the surface as they once were. If I could go back and revisit my old sexual behaviours and the way that I once viewed intimacy in comparison with how I feel right now, I would probably do away with ninety-eight percent of my sexual encounters, not because they were bad experiences, but rather they were with people with whom I had hardly any compatibility. I didn't look at the big picture in those relationships, and oftentimes we simply move into the intimate part of the relationship too fast. When you replay those old experiences in your mind, you may begin to wonder what you could have done differently, what you should have done differently, and what you probably shouldn't have done at all. But because we cannot go back and erase the past, and because the past, present, and future are one great continuum, the only thing we can do is take the lessons from those experiences, apply them to where we are now, and carry them into our next relationship. I can speak for myself and say that I am not blind; I see physically attractive men on a daily basis. I spend the majority of my time in the gym, so to me, it comes with the territory. My thoughts are, for the most part, fleeting, lasting only a few seconds before I return to my session; there is no desire to throw a man down and jump his bones. There is also no desire, on my part, to speak to someone or to initiate a conversation based purely on aesthetics. When we're young, we have a tendency to look at the physical and lose our minds. But as we get older, we start to reflect upon things of importance. We make better-informed decisions and we try our best not to repeat any mistakes from our past. This whole concept of just randomly being physical with other people not only comes off as immoral, but simply unsafe. There are an infinite number of ways that you can be harmed by allowing different people into your bed; internal damage, as well as the opportunity to increase your chances of being damaged mentally and emotionally. This goes double for women as we tend to equate sex or physical contact with love.

This pattern has been carried out by us for eons, and once we open ourselves up physically to someone, it's almost impossible to detach. Once you have taken this other person inside of you, they then become a part of you, as we are all connected to everyone and everything. Being able to detach yourself from someone emotionally, while maintaining your focus and making sound decisions, is a task. Mentally, you are all over the place, and physically, you cannot take back, or erase, what happened.

Knowing this, you want to try your best to create your intimate experiences with positivity and positive people; those whom you are most comfortable with. For me, my demisexuality only makes it easier to remain abstinent until I am ready to engage intimately with another person. Eventually, intimacy will happen, and the lessons I learned from past relationships will help me receive the right individual, at the time, that is right for me. You will, at some point, come to realize that having sex, or making love, or whatever you want to call it, is so much better when you can relate to the person you're with; when there is compatibility and complete understanding of the other person's needs and expectations. Making wise decisions regarding your behaviour, and making the right choices with respect to your higher self is very important. Those experiences become a part of you, and once the act has been committed and you finally take the time to reflect upon it, you want pleasant memories, not ones that you want to forget. As crazy as it sounds, you will run into people who mock you for not wanting to sleep around. I have been a victim of this many times, but I pride myself on being in control of who and what I allow into my space. I personally, do not have the desire to go out and be with random people; my being single is not a justification to do so. There is nothing urging me to forget my own importance, and to not consider my own feelings of worthiness. As I mentioned before, when we are young, we don't give this much thought. We are more concerned with satisfying those urges and desires than we are with the consequences of our actions. While this is not a crime, it could have an adverse effect on the way you view others, and yourself, in relation to intimacy and sex. Being aware of what you want is not something you are born with, so these mishaps and lacks of judgement have to happen; we have to learn through experience. Sometimes, it takes years for us to find that special person who we want to be intimate with, and other times, we think we've found that certain someone and it turns out that we got it all wrong. So, it is extremely important that you be mindful of what you are doing and who you share those moments with.

There is a sexual exchange of energy which occurs every single time, whether it be positive or negative, that is absorbed by each person involved. This intertwining of energies can often cause us to confuse our own feelings with the feelings of the other person, and if that person is just a random nobody or someone we may never see again, it makes it more difficult, internally, to determine what that experience was all about.

Ultimately, this just leads to more complications and a greater hesitance to be intimate again. Ever. It could also cause you to be more untrusting and unable to recognize when someone is being genuine in their efforts towards you.

I began this chapter by speaking about temptation. There will always be people and situations that tempt us, but as you become more aware of what you truly want and what you truly deserve, your ability to ignore the things that are not in alignment will strengthen. If you are progressing at a normal rate, mentally and emotionally, there should be a variance between your past and present behaviours; an improvement in your decision-making skills.

Being in love, making love, and having that person love you back, is some of the best energy you will ever experience in your life. It is the complete opposite of hopping in and out of bed with different people and, with the exception of being self-serving, I cannot, myself, see the benefits. Opening yourself up to repeated hurt is a way to anchor yourself to low self-esteem, which in turn, creates a cycle of self-inflicted pain. The desire to be numb becomes greater; it almost seems as if it is the end game.

When you choose to be single, however, your perspective changes. You become priority number one. Internally, you have binoculars on; you become more aware of everything and you are less tempted to harm yourself.

You are less inclined to do things, specifically, sexual things, which you will later regret. I am more cautious about who I let into my private spaces; my home, my bed, my heart. If I sense that a person is not good for me, I will listen to that little voice, and let my intuition take over. Having complete compatibility with someone, knowing what that person wants from you, your willingness to provide and their reciprocation, ALL while existing on a similar plane (level of thought), sounds like a dream come true. But the truth is, in fact, that if you're not on a somewhat congruent path, there will be difficult times ahead. If you cannot relate to the person that you are in a relationship with, then, honestly, what are you doing there? Why are you there pretending to relate to this person? What are you standing to gain from pretending/lying to yourself and this other person? These are only a few questions that you should ask yourself if you are ever faced with the likelihood of being by yourself.

YOU. WILL. SURVIVE. And you will come to find just how important it is to choose wisely. It is so important, and what you take away from the act of saving yourself for that particular person, is so beautiful. When you are finally intimate with someone who genuinely makes you feel comfortable and cared for, it counts as more than just some miscellaneous roll in the hay. The experience should be pleasant for both of you. There should be no pressure, on either side, to move forward into a sexual relationship if one of you is not ready. Sometimes, there is no pressure, but an underlying feeling that we have to move quickly into the bedroom in order to keep the other person interested. Big mistake. Respect yourself and demand it from your partner.

I had to learn these things through experience, and those experiences taught me to look at intimacy and sex on a much broader scale. Abstinence gives me such a better perspective, and I have begun to notice that it's (sex) all that some people think about. It works for me. I am granted more time to read, write, paint, sleep and less time on who I'm going to bed with. I actually like being in there by myself.

This may not be the case for you. You may have other outlets, other ways in which you choose to spend your time. The best part of that is you being able to choose. Whether you invite someone over or you decide to go on a romantic date or if you just want to grab your partner's hand and stare up towards the stars, remember. You control the narrative, and if things veer off from the direction in which you want them to go, pull things back together, if you like, or if not, gracefully depart yourself from the situation. Sex, at any point in time, is not an obligation. It should be a consensual moment; one you are willing to go through without being forced. It also works the other way around; seeing an attractive guy makes me wonder about his depth; the physical part is easy.

When I mention the fact that I am not sexually active, most of them find it to be very respectable, and in turn, they become more respectful of me. It's been many years now, so the challenge of trying not to sleep with people has all but disappeared. Physical appearance is simply not enough to trigger me back into old behaviours. If you are with me at this level, then you can agree that little things like "looks" have been left somewhere back on mile two. We have gone way beyond that. We still have to be mindful, though, as not to put ourselves into difficult situations. And, of course, having respect for ourselves is most important overall. There is no harm in you taking the time to figure out what it is you truly want. Take as long as you want, and as long as you need to. As willing as you are to give of yourself, he or she should be just as willing to do the same.

Chapter Six

Falling in Love with Yourself

Love is in the air. It is a small word which means something to each and every one of us; it is a part of what drives some of us to do the things that we do while simultaneously being the exact thing that causes some of us to run away. It can be flighty and robust, passionate and pessimistic, both beautiful and blinding. But when we speak about the love we have for ourselves, we tend to talk about our love for the material things we've attained, or for something that exists outside of our physical bodies. We love our houses and our cars, the brand-new pair of shoes we recently purchased, and that hot new ticket item that we just had to have. While there is nothing wrong with buying brand new shoes or dressing up our homes, it's important to understand that those things will eventually cease to give you the "loving" feeling that you had at that particular moment. They are, in fact, extensions of us; what our body is craving as a means of satisfaction; a temporary fix. These "things" bring us joy, and joy is good, right? It feels good, it makes us smile, and we want this feeling all of the time. So, we buy more things as a way of continuing this joy, and as a way to avoid the idea that we may, in fact, feel less than by not piling on "things" as a testament to how much we love ourselves and how happy we can be. This is exactly the reason why we are told that money cannot buy love or happiness; these two things reside within us. Money and material things actually create a sense of security and comfortability. They can make life easier or harder for us, depending on who we are, and enable us to live a more stable life. But what about the person who doesn't have these things? Are they endowed with a lessened ability to know true joy and happiness?

I want to touch on the concept of having a true sense of inner joy and the importance of loving yourself in spite of having, or not having, "things" be the reason why you do so. Knowing your worth plays a major role in how you allow others to treat you, as well as how you value yourself, and how you treat others. Being able to love someone unconditionally is very difficult, but this is, in fact, how you should love yourself all the time. It has nothing to do with your outside appearance; technology has allowed us to alter that if, and whenever, we choose. Falling in love with yourself is simply the act of loving yourself without condition. Your attributes, your character, the way you treat yourself and other people, not causing any harm, having compassion and empathy, being grateful and appreciative, being kind to yourself, fulfilling your life purpose, respecting everyone and everything. These are just a few elements of what loving yourself means.

When you love yourself from the inside out, it radiates from within and is noticeable by those around you. Time and time again, we are shown images of self-hatred; violence, racism, murder. These things all stem from a lack of self-love because it is impossible to give someone something that you do not have yourself. In other words, if I do not love myself, I can't give that love to anyone else.

This makes it easy for someone to commit a heartless crime and not have their conscious be affected. The same thing holds true when we are talking about knowing our worth in regards to being single or being in a relationship. Loving yourself wholeheartedly enables you to make sound decisions. You automatically know what you want from the other person; how you want to be treated, touched, and talked to. You have a better sense of what role you are playing and you refuse to settle for anything less than that. If you are choosing to be single, like me, then you are already aware of the role you are playing. You're not playing at all. I'm extremely focused on my work, and I'm constantly moving toward becoming the greatest version of myself. But this inner joy and love and peace are all possible because I know my worth, and it is not dependent upon whether or not someone else loves me; it is self-sufficient. Learning to do this is a task, and you will have to experience heartache many times over in order to get the full gist of it. We are taught that love is a thing; an object, like a book or a shoe. In order to love myself, and to love others correctly, I had to unlearn that. Love is something that you do; it's an action. When we tell someone, "I love you", love is the verb. We are "acting" out our love. It is not something that you can actually place in someone's hand like a book or a shoe, so why, then, do we assume that it is a thing? When you show your love, you perform an act of something; you cannot literally "show" it. You have to exude it, and when you reach the highest peak of love, you will have become it. It will be the reason why you do everything that you do, and all other reasons will become futile. Every morning I wake up with an abundance of love in my heart for myself and for others, even those who I've never met. We all have the capacity to feel this way, to love one another as we love ourselves. It is something that we should tap into more often. But first, we must learn how to truly love and care for ourselves. We have to nurture those hidden parts within us, those parts that others neglect to see as important, as well as those parts that we, ourselves, have tucked away from the possibility of being healed. As human beings, we expect to be loved by other human beings. We expect to be cared for by others, and we expect that we will be comforted in such a way that pleases us. However, as we grow and gain a better understanding of how those expectations can, and do, eventually change, we learn the importance of falling in love with ourselves, and that no one owes us the love that we should already possess inside.

We all do things that we aren't proud of at one time or another, so we need to acknowledge our wrongdoings first. We need to apologize to ourselves just as we would to whomever we've wronged. We also need to promise ourselves that we will refrain from self-inflicted pain; we need to make a verbal promise that we will do our best to protect our own value and self-worth.

Old wounds can be healed in the same fashion. Sitting down with yourself and peeling back the layers of hurt and neglect from the past will make it easier for you to tackle any new feelings which may have risen to the surface. Once you do this for yourself, and once the healing begins, you will have learned to love on an entirely different level. You will become more mindful of the pain that others feel, and you will become more sensitive because of your own experiences. Self-love will slowly take the place of those painful experiences, and the way that others treat you will become very significant. You won't accept any forms of disrespect or mistreatment, and you, in turn, will reciprocate that level of respect to others. Even when others DO say things that rub you the wrong way, you are mindful of how you react, and you see their behaviour as something they are dealing with internally as opposed to something you caused them to do. When this happens, I feel overwhelmingly empathetic to their situation, and I don't take it personally. Oddly enough, I actually feel more love for them and I try to see if there is something I can do to help. This kind of love can be learned despite the fact that we are mostly taught to cater to our own egos; "I, me, my", or "Do you, and I'll do me." We are indoctrinated to believe that no one is more important than we are, so therefore, if what we want does not benefit US, then we don't put forth the extra effort. BUT we fail to implement the same energy into taking care of our internal selves. We allow others to abuse us mentally, emotionally, and spiritually. We inflict a lot of this abuse upon ourselves as well. So, it comes down to whether or not you even feel that falling in love with yourself is important. If it is, you take the necessary steps to move forward into a higher dimension of reality; a better way of viewing the world and what truly matters. If it doesn't strike your interest, then you may be somewhat masochistic in nature, or you have yet to reach the point of pain that triggers you into change.

    I will tell you, from personal experience, that having this love of self has illuminated my journey in every way imaginable. Every aspect of being alone has been made easier, and I'm not concerned at all about when that "special someone" will enter my life. I'm completely focused on helping others who may be having a much harder time with all of this. It is not easy, but if you are committed to doing the work, you CAN get to the place of inner love that you seek.

Chapter Seven

Understanding and Embracing Your Journey

Accepting who you are and your journey into this single lifestyle; how do we do this? Some may see it as a thing of spontaneity, or as a way for you to garner attention. Because you know this is not the case, you choose to move forward with the idea that you are doing something for the betterment of yourself, and something that makes sense to you. It's the flowering of your own truth. It's also an amazing feeling to be able to ignore society's push and pull with regard to how you choose to stand in that truth; to know that you are in control of what it is you want to do. It is indeed possible that you being able to choose could bring you back to the person that you were always meant to be; the leader of your own marching band. As you move forward every day, into this, you will find that it is a good thing, and not as complex as you once thought it would be. Being able to embrace your journey; being able to accept your "singleness".

That is, however, how we come into this world; a single, solitary individual on a journey to find his or her purpose; a purpose which is not always what others expect or feel it should be. We all have something that we are destined to do. Some of us are destined for absolute greatness. Some of us are destined to live our lives over again and again if you believe in such a thing, repeating this life cycle until we've got it right. And if coming here to this planet and agreeing to live this life purpose is something that we all do, there should not be a problem when someone chooses to not be in the company of others as a way of achieving this contractual thing. This is especially true when you have experienced so much in so little time because life is not something that lasts for a billion years; not this earthly life or this physical body that we have. It is not imperishable. It eventually deteriorates and fades away. So, for the time that we have here, it's important that we are able to accept the choices we've made, learn the lessons when those choices don't serve us correctly and be able to adjust ourselves according to how we truly want our journey to go. How I feel about time; it's just an illusion. It is something that forces us to focus on everything except the present moment. And when we accept this illusion to be just that, we are then given the opportunity to live in the moment; to create and to decipher this purpose and to give it our undivided attention. When we figure it all out, and we acknowledge the truth of why we are here, we should then combine everything that we know, and that should motivate us to get busy. What we have to say, what we have to do on this earth; if it is meant to be seen and felt by others, we should strive to put it out there. Time, in this sense, is of the essence. If we are to accomplish this thing, we should then be more aware of what's going on around us; if fulfilling your soul's purpose really matters. Embracing where we are now is so very important, as is remembering that we are all special in our own way. Like I said before, some of us are born to do great things, and it may sometimes take us forever to figure out what that great thing is, but when we reach the point of knowing that we are not just here, that we exist for a certain purpose, we should then accept it and take the necessary steps to gradually move into it.

Of course, not everyone will figure this out before leaving this physical plane. However, those of us who know what it is we should be doing, and are actually doing it, are pleased that that part of us wishes to come out; that part of us that wants to be heard, and needs to be known. So, this journey of being single and being happy is not dependent on whether or not you EVER find that special someone. If you leave this earth and you never come into union with anyone else, you know that you have made the choice to do what it is you want to do. However, you are afforded to do it, it is done by your own rules and not by how society dictates it should be. We grow up believing that "we must do this" and "we must do that", and that life will be much harder if we decide to stray from the pack. I can tell you from experience that life has been harder trying to live by those societal ideologies. I've had my most exciting and memorable moments while I was alone and able to focus, able to clear my head, able to meditate, able to walk through nature, able to just sit and not have someone try and tell me how I should navigate throughout my own journey. This moment of being by yourself; just be happy about it. I know that might sound crazy to some and most will find it impossible to do, but it is much easier than you think. You simply walk forward; take your steps just like you would step into anything else. There's not much of a difference.

For instance, when you walk into a room full of strangers, you may feel a little bit of anxiety because you are not completely sure of how things will go, but ultimately, you are in control of how things go and how you choose to react. There is a sigh of relief that comes from knowing that you are the one manning the ship and that you are setting out in the direction that you want to go. And when you notice that you are moving in the wrong direction, you have the ability to look at where you went wrong and fix it. This is your opportunity to figure out who it is you want to be, what it is you're meant to do, and why you matter.

This journey is something else; you most certainly will lose the desire to do a lot of things that were once important to you. Your focus will change and you will come to the conclusion that you can have an amazing life without being romantically or intimately attached to another human being. For me, life is more about learning and absorbing as much positive energy as I possibly can, and then exuding that onto others. Relationships happen, and people either choose to stick around or disappear.

Knowing that makes it easier to accept my singleness; my existence, my happiness, is not based on the choices that others make. When that realization hits you, the desire to step into your purpose will increase and will be almost impossible for you to ignore. Being by yourself will allow you to focus more, and when you have reached a point where you have made your purpose known, and have fulfilled it to the best of your abilities, you may ultimately want to go into union with someone. It is my hope that you will have a better understanding of what it is you're doing, unlike myself when I decided to get married all those years ago. I was not fulfilling my purpose; I knew that there was something more that I should have been doing. I did not realize, back then, that I needed to get some time alone with myself so that I could figure out what that "something" was. I was so consumed with fixing marital problems and trying to learn who my spouse was, while simultaneously pushing down my own personal goals, my creativity, and everything that I wanted to achieve. Eventually, this other person became my priority.

Some people believe that, when you are married, you should never put yourself first, that it's a selfish thing to do. But there is a balance which needs to be kept, and oftentimes, we are not taught how to create that balance. Some of us, as children, were not fortunate enough to experience that sense of balance in our parents' lives either. Therefore, they were unable to pass that along to us. It is something that we as individuals have to find, and when we can't find it or have a lack of understanding, our marriages tend to reflect that. To be completely honest, at a certain point in my marriage, I grew tired of it. I wanted to, I needed to; I felt like I was in quicksand. I needed to get back to who I was as a person, and I needed to nurture myself; I needed to nourish myself with the things that would allow me to grow into my purpose. It's so important to do this once you become aware of it. Choosing to ignore it is synonymous with smothering yourself. I have no desire to put myself back in that position ever again. It was a position of feeling completely enclosed. I could not sprout. I could not blossom. I could not grow. I felt like I was in a box which was meant to hold me down and contort my being; coming out of my shell was almost unheard of. I was starting to become a shell of myself. Where I am now is where I was meant to be. Focused, working, and waking up every morning with my purpose on my mind. It took a long time for me to get to this point, so when we go back to the concept of time, there was a lot of time wasted doing other things besides what I am doing now, which is living. Actually LIVING, not just being alive but living, and thriving, and striving toward my purpose for being on this planet. If you are in this position of feeling trapped, whether it be a marriage or a relationship that you know is not healthy, or in any situation where you feel like you aren't allowed to be who it is you are meant to be, you should not stay there and be stifled. It is heartbreaking to look back at your life and know that you can't get that time back. When you figure out what it is you're supposed to do, you should embrace that wholeheartedly and not allow anyone to make you believe that what you want to do is unimportant. This is your path, what others think should have little to no significance. This is your life to live. Embrace that the very moment you realize that it exists. I have known my purpose ever since fifth grade. I was told that I should be a writer. I had dreams, however, of becoming an aeronautical engineer. Ignoring my gut instincts, I pushed the military aside to date the man I would eventually end up marrying. Words cannot express how much I regret that. I didn't follow my dreams of being an engineer OR getting into what I knew was my purpose; writing and inspiring others with my own personal experiences, and my own journey. Helping others understand the importance of self-love matters a great deal to me. You need to know that being single, and/or being alone, is not a bad thing. It is, in fact, a gateway to finding out what you truly want and what you truly need. It's also an opportunity to get away from the ideas of others so that you can reflect and recognize those wants and needs without all of the chatter. As I mentioned earlier, coming to terms with who you are is not something that happens overnight. Life happens, and it sometimes takes us off of our intended path. When taking all of these things into consideration, you can see why it is so important to seize these opportunities when they are presented to us. Also, in those moments of disconnect, you will be able to get back to yourself and recapture that feeling. I cannot express this enough.

When you know what you should be doing, and you are moving forward consistently and doing it, it is a feeling of pure bliss. It is a feeling that no one can take away, as well as one that becomes extremely urgent. When you wake up every morning and you just HAVE to satisfy that urge, there can be no doubt that it is your divine purpose. You begin to embrace every moment you have to develop your craft, and every single one of those moments matters. Once this happens, you lose all interest in the concept of time because what you are doing is what you love to do, what you were meant to do. You will have reached the point where you can actually take your time, nothing can throw you off anymore. In your heart, mind, and spirit, you know your truth, so it becomes easier to block out those things that are not conducive to your happiness or your journey. You can then, finally, begin to enjoy your life here on this earth. You can fully begin to love yourself and others. You can finally stop worrying now, because honestly, what is the root cause of all worrying? Not being sure of one's self and/or the decisions that one must make, second-guessing and not trusting your intuition. This becomes a thing of the past once you recognize who you are. There is no longer a mystery, and your discovery brings about a long-awaited moment of peace. I cannot think of anything better than becoming the greatest version of myself. My being single has only propelled me forward into fulfilling my soul's desire. One day, I may meet Mister Right or maybe not. I am okay with either outcome. You will be okay too because, in the end, you will be a better person for yourself. You will amaze and fascinate yourself with what you are able to accomplish when uncertainty is no longer a factor. I am so glad to be where I am right now; able to live fully in my purpose and not worry about the past. It is the present that matters most for me. Now is what's relevant.

Hopefully, you will one day figure this out for yourself, and life will begin to show you the glimpse of heaven that you dream of.

Chapter Eight

What Else is There Besides Sex?

Over the course of my journey, I have come to find that sex is less and less of an issue. Understanding the concept of what sex is, and the importance of withholding that from the equation until you have some idea of what you are doing in a relationship, despite what you may think, really matters. Even if a relationship is not what you're looking for, the idea of having random sex with random people at random times, in this day and time, is simply unappealing. My beliefs regarding this are partly due to my age. I am forty-six years old. This also lends to my having a better understanding of promiscuity, as well as knowing what a person my age tends to look for in a potential partner. Also, regardless of age, we all know the risks that come along with casual sex. Not everyone equates having sex with love. Not everyone equates sex with the concept of "no strings attached."

I can say from personal experience that it is very easy to misconstrue sexual experiences and their relevancy. When you lie down with someone and they have their own mindset/agenda about what that particular experience is for them, it may not be congruent with what you have in mind. Sex, in itself, to me, is very sacred. In my younger years, I did not have that sentiment, I did not have that awareness, I did not know the importance of restraint. As I have mentioned before, it is an exchange of energy. So, when you put yourself into a position where you are constantly having sex with random people, you are absorbing all of their energies. I won't say that everyone you sleep with is filled with negative energy, but having an abundance of "purposeless" sex opens the door for a lot of misunderstanding.

The title of this chapter really speaks to the fact that there are tons of other things to do outside of having sex. I know of so many people who have this "sexual" mindset; it seems to be all they think about. For me, personally, being single has actually curtailed many of the thoughts and beliefs I once had about sex and intimacy as a whole. At this point in time, for me, it has no relevance. There is so much more to life that I want to explore and discover about myself so much more than crawling into bed with someone. That hardly takes any effort; a couple of drinks and just the right amount of coercion. Choosing this journey comes with its pros and cons, but not having sex all the time is surprisingly not that difficult. I have come to understand that as we grow older and begin to long for companionship, it becomes more about intimacy and having that person who supports you, and loves you unconditionally. That person who complements you and is conducive to your happiness. With that said, I do not feel that my being single is a pass for me to go out and sleep with whomever and whenever I want. I know that is often said about single people and their sexual "freedom." Don't believe the hype. Not having sex allows me to have more focus when it comes to other aspects of my life. When you are on the path of enlightenment and finding out who you are, you will find that most things that meant a lot to you in the past are of less importance. There are a lot of things that will eventually fall away, and some of those things may be sexual in nature; what turned you on in the past may no longer trigger a sexual reaction. Over time, you will come to see that random sexual acts mean nothing; they don't enhance your livelihood, intelligence, or well-being. You had sex. Okay. Now what? It's a temporary feeling, and if it's a temporary feeling which gets you high, it can easily be considered an addiction. I am grateful for the things in my life that add a sense of value and worth, and while that may indeed be sex for some people, it is not for me. While it is looked upon as a part of life, my life is not hinged upon whether or not I sleep with someone today, tomorrow, or two weeks from now. I get my "high" from working out or walking in nature or waking up and going for an early morning run. I get that "high" when I accomplish a goal that I've set for myself. My intention here is not to demonize sex. It is not to make you feel bad. My intention is to solely get you to think before you act and to make sure that you understand the bigger picture with regard to your sexual interactions with others. I want to remind you that how you feel matters. Having control over your emotions and the situation matters. I would REALLY like to have this chapter be an account of my personal experience with sex so that you can bounce your own feelings off of mine. I want it to trigger you and make you look at your true sexual self, and inspire you to heal any wounds that come up to the surface. My honest and pure feeling about sex right now is this: If it happens, it happens. If it doesn't, it doesn't. You may or may not feel the same as me, but my being transparent is very important to the message I am trying to convey to you. I love the fact that I am in control of the situation. I am in control of myself, at all times. I am much wiser sexually and feel absolutely no pressure to please the desires of others. MY pleasure is what matters now, MY happiness is what matters now, MY peace of mind is what matters now. These are things that I refuse to trade on, and OMG, especially not for sex. What you will find out on this journey is that there are an infinite number of ways to become stimulated, and that sex will not always be the foundation of that stimulation. You will begin to notice all the little things that you've managed to overlook that were once pleasurable to you. A warm, relaxing bath… a few moments of introspection… looking at the stars in a moonlit sky. These are just a few things that I, myself, pay more attention to now, things that help promote a better sense of well-being. I can go on and on, but the truth of the matter is that random/casual sex can begin to wear you down physically, emotionally, mentally, and spiritually. And while the urge to hop into bed has increased over time, the urge to be smart and more selective seems to have little to no bearing. Being smart and using good judgement is NOT a bad thing. Having discernment over your personal choices regarding sex is a GREAT thing. As I mentioned at the very beginning of this chapter, don't believe the hype. Becoming aware of your higher self and honoring that is much more satisfying. Realizing your purpose and why you are here, and walking in that direction is much more satisfying. Of course, these are only my opinions, and they directly reflect my lifestyle and journey, but my overall intention is to open your mind to a different perspective.

Labeling myself sexually, I would have to define myself as demisexual; I am not drawn to anyone sexually until AFTER some kind of strong, emotional connection has taken place. Couple that with my introversion, and... But I am perfectly fine with the consequences involved. My sexuality is something that I am not afraid to share with others, and it really began to take its roots at the end of my last relationship, almost seven years ago. Ever since then, energy exchange has become both important and unimportant to me, meaning that, while I care about who I sleep with, I don't care if I sleep with anyone at all.

Sex, for me, has altogether taken on a whole new meaning from what it used to be. It actually makes me want to be more cautious and conscious in my thinking. It triggers my intuition and I pay closer attention to how that makes me feel during my decision-making process. Honestly, I am grateful for the internal growth that has occurred over the years. I don't feel stagnated or that I have missed out on anything with regard to sex. I have grown so much internally, and have garnered so much unconditional love for myself throughout this journey. No one has the power to control my desires anymore; only I can do that. Having that level of control over myself is, in fact, empowering within itself. Putting it out there that singleness is not synonymous with sadness or salaciousness, is one of my missions. Taking this break is going to allow you to form a better relationship with yourself, so don't feel bad for choosing yourself over the needs of others. Go do something healthy... breathe... meditate... read... rest. These are all much healthier alternatives when compared to promiscuity. Also, as women, we have so many delicate energies swirling around within us. We should always treat ourselves as if we are a prize, not to be won, but to be earned. I honestly believe that "feeling like a flower" is a more beautiful feeling to have. Who wouldn't want to be treasured on all levels? And even when you are single and not being actively pursued, you should treasure yourself. I can think of a million things I would rather do besides lying naked underneath someone who doesn't truly care about me. My peace of mind and my higher self and my moral compass will just not allow that to happen anymore. Being single will definitely make you more observant and less afraid to voice your opinions about what you're willing to deal with sexually, and what steps you are willing to take to implement those boundaries. You will find that sex is not a coping mechanism, but rather a sacred act not to be shared with everyone. You won't need it to be happy. You won't be heartbroken over your lack of sexual activity. You definitely will not be desperate. What WILL happen within you is the acquirement of a new mindset. So, to answer the question, unapologetically, WHAT ELSE IS THERE BESIDES SEX? EVERYTHING... If you choose to continue along this journey, just like I decided to years ago, you will see how little importance this issue holds at the end of the day. I cannot say when that "aha" moment will hit you, but when it does, you're truly going to be thankful for the revelation.

Chapter Nine

Positivity In, Negativity Out

The whole point of this choice that you're making is to be your true, authentic self. You can always choose to do otherwise, but as far as your journey is concerned, and depending on the level of progression you're wanting for yourself, where is that really going to take you? Where are you going to end up? Being single is a choice, so there is nothing wrong with choosing that. It is where you learn to be strong and stand firm in your beliefs, and also, where you grasp the importance of becoming an independent, individualistic human being. It's okay to be alone, despite the many fears had by those in today's society. For me, it invokes a certain level of power and a better understanding of who I want to be. Of course, I'm not saying that this can't be achieved while in a relationship, but before a relationship even has the chance to take form, you should know the importance of who you are and what you bring to the table. This journey has many paths, and many avenues… many turns and plenty of speed bumps and dead ends. But a dead-end does not automatically mean your journey has ended; you can simply choose to turn around and go back to what feels familiar. We sometimes take the wrong steps, and it's not always easy to admit when those steps are wrong. But that's okay. That's you being human, and that's you course correcting. You won't be able to avoid EVERY pothole on the road and to be completely honest, the road is set up in such a way that it teaches you the value of knowing when to take the alternate route. It often provides the "flashing lights" which warn you of impending danger. Pretty soon, you'll get a gist of what it is that promotes positivity and happiness within you, and what does not. Being alone in your singleness will begin to heighten your awareness of what adds to your progression, and what stagnates it, what drives your passion and what makes you feel stagnated. Distractions will rear their ugly heads and you will know what to do with that energy. You will easily spot the negativity of others, how they view you and your decision to choose yourself. I say, choose yourself at every turn. Not to the point that you alienate those you care for, but when it's time to choose what's best for your upward movement, choose you. Once you do this, you will be able to see who is really cheering for you; they will encourage you to keep moving forward, to do what makes you happy, and they won't make you feel like you're doing something to them. Staying positive and incorporating healthy lifestyle habits will only further increase your ability to stay uplifted throughout your journey. You are choosing to love and nurture yourself, and choosing to save yourself for someone that you deem worthy of all you have to offer. As I said, I'm not trying to be an advocate for abstinence or promote some weird sexual-withholding phenomena. That's not what this book is about. This is simply my effort to get you to understand that you are more than what you see when you're standing in the mirror, and you are more than what others see when they look at you. Even when you are standing there by yourself, it is okay to be standing there by yourself. You have to understand that standing next to someone is not necessary in order for you to be happy. I'm bursting with happiness and I am grateful that I have that choice. Once upon a time, I did not have that freedom. Like most people, I used to think that I needed someone else to create happiness for me. Little did I know that making myself happy would be one of the greatest successes of my life. Eliminating the negativity wasn't always easy, nor was it easy to accept the task of remembering to stay positive in the face of challenges. The latter has indeed paid off, and now I am observant of everything and everyone. I find myself now, standing up for those who are afraid to be alone. I AM an advocate for that. Whatever brings you to the point of singleness is your business, so don't ever let anyone tell you that you can't be happy this way. You most certainly can be; I know that I am. I am the happiest that I've ever been, and as far as a physical relationship is concerned, it's also the longest I have been without one. My happiness is not predicated on whether or not someone is in my life. You need to know that being with someone will never fulfill you if you, yourself, have not internally gotten your shit together. Pardon my words, but they are facts. You have to work on EVERY aspect of yourself, and a big part of that is ridding your life of negative people, places, and things; whatever you find yourself addicted to that eventually perpetuates self-harm.

    You also need to know that you will be perfectly fine by yourself. Your beautiful self… your intelligent self… your strong self… your self-assured self. At the end of each and every day, who you are inside is what matters, and what you believe to be of importance to you carries a lot of weight. Choosing this course is nobody else's business and that is the only way I know how to put it. Remain positive, and be happy now. While you're reading this, you can go ahead and choose happiness; single and happy? Imagine that. And if you are married and you don't want to be married anymore, I can tell you from personal experience, don't stay there. You deserve happiness, and sometimes that means starting over with the hopes of regaining a sense of your life's purpose and repositioning yourself on your chosen path. Before you attempt to get upset with me, let me say that I am NOT telling you to get a divorce. I am, however, telling you to fall face-first into whatever adds happiness, joy, and longevity to your life. Your reality is created by you and your perception of the things that surround you on a daily basis. For instance, when you see a tree, of course, you did not create that tree. However, the thoughts and emotions that are triggered by seeing the tree are all YOUR thoughts and emotions. That also means that someone else can come along, see that same tree, and have a totally different perception than you, thereby creating TWO different realities. With that being said, you not only create how you feel each day, but you also allow other people to manipulate and dictate that reality. You should make a pact with yourself and agree not to let that happen again. I fell prey to this myself by staying in relationships way longer than I should have. And though I learned valuable lessons from those relationships, they just simply lasted too long. I was unhappy, and feeling miserable and obligated while pretending and suppressing all of MY wants and desires, suppressing my gifts because they didn't fit into the equation of what my partner wanted. You would be wise not to put your dreams and aspirations away for anyone. There is no way for you to welcome positivity while remaining an open vessel for negativity.

Being by yourself, at times, is how you gain an understanding of what those positive and negative things are. It's also how you construct a plan of implementation. This is not as hard as you think. It's simply a choice, and we are given the opportunity to make these choices every single day. At the end of the day, we hope that those wise choices will help to welcome positive consequences. The true gem is that even if they do garner negative results, there are valuable lessons tucked away within them that can be used to promote a healthier sense of well-being. You just have to be willing to learn and embrace what the universe is trying to tell you.

Chapter Ten

A New and Improved You

We all have our own individual stories and ways of doing things, and how those choices stand to shape us into form is purely based on what direction we want to go in. Setting out on an intentional path of singleness is a great way to get started on self-improvement. You're choosing to take a different route as a means of "getting it right this time." And why wouldn't you want to make life easier for yourself? This is the perfect time to give yourself permission to open up to new perspectives and to possibly relearn who you are. Being able to do what I want, when I want, is absolutely amazing. But I didn't just wake up one day with that mindset; I had to relearn that THAT was actually an option that I could have. Learning that helped me to better improve my decision-making skills and it left me with the understanding that MY life belongs to me, and that I don't have to feel guilty about not catering to others. You, too, will begin to understand the value of YOUR life; it was not given to you with the intention of you NOT living it for yourself. If I could go back… I know that this is probably how you feel about your situation at times as well. But, hey, you can fix whatever you feel is broken about it whenever you are ready. In other words, don't feel bad about coulda, woulda, shoulda's. Take this opportunity to get to know yourself and to improve upon yourself as you see fit. Fix yourself and prepare your potential partner for the gift of receiving you at your very best. I truly feel that someone deserves that from me, and I can only hope that person feels I'm worthy of the same. Whoever he is, I can only hope that he is somewhere, right now, preparing himself for me. And if that just happens to not be the case at all, I've grown to learn acceptance of that. So, while I'm saying be single for as long as you need to be, I'm also saying that when you're ready to partner up with someone, don't sacrifice all that you've learned and experienced just to do so. You have to remain aware of where you want to go in YOUR life, even if you are dating. The moment you become engulfed in that person's dreams and desires to the extent of forfeiting your own, the cycle of losing yourself just starts right back up again. It will be up to you to create that balance between flexibility and vigilance. Like I said, being by yourself will allow you the time to fine-tune what needs repairing, as well as determining why you're truly here. I believe that we are all here to do something meaningful, and with purpose, something fascinating. We just have to find out what it is. A new and improved version of yourself is just waiting to be unveiled. More than likely, someone has decided to stick around to see what becomes of you and your newness. They're probably not sure what the hell is going on with you, but they want to see how you end up after all of this. LOL… people just have to see shit. When I began writing this book, I wasn't sure if I would ever finish because I was, and still am, in a constant state of learning myself and what it is I want. I am open to improvement, every day, every moment, and engaged with what's important to me. I'm really tapped in and focused on myself; I'm a priority to myself. I know in my heart that what I'm doing and saying is not in vain. My purpose is to help others understand the importance of self-preservation, while simultaneously sparing themselves bullshit-ridden relationships. I am driven to also help others recognize that it's perfectly fine to be by themselves sometimes, and to stand up and say, "Okay, I've had enough of the 'settling'." I had to do the work as well. Ultimately, the moment you accept that only you can create happiness for yourself will be the moment you stop blaming others for where you are in your own life. You are responsible for your own failures, so you may as well accept and embrace them for the lessons they brought you. Embrace them, utilize them, and move forward. Acceptance helps to promote healing, and healing is the same as recovery. Recover and realign yourself; improve and initiate a new beginning. Hold yourself accountable for the steps you take from here on out. Forgive yourself for stumbling, and for not understanding the importance of this before now. You are going to be stronger, make wiser choices, not want to hurt yourself, and surround yourself with people and things that help to propel you towards your goals. I find that this is much easier for me to do when I am by myself; you may see things differently, and that is okay. Nothing I have said this entire time is something that you'd BETTER do. I am merely sharing with you what has worked for me in the past, as well as in the present, to help me gain a greater understanding of myself and what I want, and need to do for myself. I am better able to channel my energy towards my work when I'm by myself. But hey, as I said, that's just me. I've learned so much about myself, so I cannot fathom apologizing for making myself unavailable. Neither should you. I'm not in a relationship at this moment because I choose not to be. I walked away from a job after putting in twelve years of hard, unappreciated work. I chose that as well, and I have no regrets because those instances, along with so many others, have led to my current level of self-improvement. At some point, your level of uncertainty must be outweighed by your willingness to take that leap of faith. After I left my job, I had no idea what I would do; how I would sustain myself. I was in school at the time, so I was juggling, as most people find themselves doing as they grow older. But even though I was searching for balance and some form of stability, I held on to that feeling in my gut; the feeling that constantly told me that I would be okay, no matter what. I thank the universe for the gift of hindsight and intuition. And when it comes to you making the choice to improve upon yourself, by all means, do it with as much fierceness as you possibly can because the "do-overs" aren't always going to come your way. Whenever the awareness of who you are and who you want to be hits you, take advantage of knowing and go after it. Prove yourself wrong. Let go of any negative self-talk, relinquish the opinions of every naysayer, and flourish unapologetically.

Chapter Eleven

Opening Your Heart to Abundance

When was the last time you looked into the mirror, or your mind's eye, and uttered the words, "I am enough?" You have to know that you are enough, that you are not lacking in your capabilities of loving yourself, loving others, and being open to the abundance you so rightly deserve. I think that sometimes we run into situations or people who make us believe that we are not worthy of more, and so when we are faced with having more, we are reluctant to grab hold of it. We then grow accustomed to not having those things, and then the "lack" thereof becomes the norm. This is why it's so important to love yourself authentically. Your heart is most open when you are aware of love in its purest form, and with this opening comes the gift of abundance. There was a shift in my thought process about five years ago. I was moved to observe the things and people in my life a little bit differently, and in doing so, my perspective on all things was dramatically changed. I grew to understand that putting myself before others was not selfish, but rather a means of self-preservation and self-care. While I still do things for others, I learned how to create boundaries which prevent the feeling of obligation that overwhelms on a personal/internal level. I also learned the power of saying NO. It doesn't make you a mean person, it clearly reminds you of the boundaries you've set for yourself and others. I say all of these things to get you to understand that when you set boundaries, you are less inclined to be stressed, and more open to giving and receiving love at a greater capacity. And this love will not be restricted to just people, but you will love everything around you. Nature, animals, the sun and the stars and the moon... you will love waking up every day. You will even love the way that other people love each other. All of this will just create more opportunities for more love and abundance over time. Of course, this does not mean that you won't ever be pissed about anything, but even then, you will see those instances with more compassion than contempt. You will have an overall better sense of clarity concerning all situations that seek to take you out of alignment.

    My being single, I have just accepted the fact that the universe wants me all to itself; it is shaping me, molding me, and preparing me for something phenomenal. It is teaching me unconditional love and pulling back the layers of my heart, as widely as possible, and pouring more love in there, and in turn, that love spills over and out of my pores into everything and onto everyone that I touch. Sounds so mushy, but whoever I choose to deal with relationship-wise will certainly be loved the way that I have learned to love myself. The passion fueling my purpose has increased because I truly love what I do. I do not write because of financial struggles or because I want to reach a certain level of fame. I write because it has always been a part of me and because my message may bring about a change for someone who truly needs it. And getting that message out without having anyone hindering the process makes my life SO much easier. I write because I truly believe that it is my purpose. I get excited about it; I wake up thinking about how to improve upon what I wrote the day before. It is who I am when I push all the noise and the bullshit aside. Believing in reincarnation, yes, I do believe that I have done this (writing) before because it's as effortless as breathing. It always has been, from the first moment I can remember picking up a pencil. With an open heart, you too will gain a better sense of what it is you were meant to do. Quiet all the ideals of what you've been told that you were supposed to be doing for a minute or two, and travel, if you can, to the center of your being, and bring your passion to the surface. What do you see? What do you feel when that thing emerges? Why have you suppressed it? How can you, little by little, interject it into your life so that you can at least say you tried? Honestly, I think you can have it; fulfil your purpose AND live abundantly and authentically. You may not make a dime doing what you love. You may become a huge success. But if it's your true calling, you won't care either way. It's more about having this urgency inside of you that you have to get out, regardless of how it might be received. You have got to have that love inside of you as well because giving yourself is how you're able to continue forward. I have never met a happy, loving, and generous person with a stick up their ass before, who makes speeches about how to be more happy, loving, and generous. And if they are walking around like that, I imagine that the stick just keeps digging deeper and deeper until they decide to be real with themselves. Without getting into the Law of Attraction too much, I will just say that whatever you ditch out, be prepared to see it heaped up on your doorstep, that goes for both the good and the bad. I think that you should stop suppressing your dreams and desires, and I also think that, if you must, make it a brief pause. Don't let them die. And by all means, don't let anybody else play the suppressor. Personally, I feel like your increased love for yourself will leave no room for those who fail to see the importance of what you're trying to create. And unlike some people, your purpose will never leave you, so dream bigger if you have to. This dream inside of me… it pounds at me… It wants to make its presence known, and I have yet to date ONE person who understands this. If you are single like me, embrace this solitary time for as long as it takes you to know that you are ready to invite someone else in. Seriously get your shit together, because when you do, you will easily detect when someone else has not, and it will save you so… much… energetically. Six years have been much easier, for me, being by myself. I am thriving, I am happy, and it hasn't curtailed anything I've wanted to achieve. I AM enough… YOU are enough… WE'RE gonna be just fine.

Chapter Twelve

Reflection and Introspection

I started working on this project about a year ago, and what I have managed to do over the course of that time is to observe how things could possibly change; if I would have to go back and edit or eat my words. Nope. What I HAVE found is more clarity and reassurance in the relevance of my message. The need for more self-love has become more apparent, and the ability to go inward needs to be of greater importance. Reflection and introspection are both beneficial in the process of self-discovery and figuring out why you're here. Whether or not that happens during meditation or prayer, connecting with nature, or just being alone and sitting still, is completely up to you. I spend a lot of time alone, so those moments of solitude work best for me. I hope that while reading this book, you were able to take what resonated with you and apply it to your personal life experiences.

I also hope that I didn't come across as too "preachy" for that will NEVER be my intention. What I wanted to give you was the understanding of just how important your feelings are regarding being alone, regardless of why you want that to be. But even more than that, I want you to learn how to love yourself unconditionally despite your past; the mistakes, the misjudgements, the "not-so-smart" behaviours. Love yourself enough to forgive yourself for it all so that you are able to move forward for your own sake and sanity. For me, this has been another year of singleness. Being able to observe others through a set of more awakened eyes has just helped to narrow things down relationship-wise; I'm STILL not willing to settle for just anyone. I am currently not engaging in any sexual or intimate activity, and I feel absolutely fine with that. I have not found anyone to be deserving of my time, energy, or my body, and I don't feel that I have to apologize for that. That is why I always stress the importance of knowing your worth. Incorporating the act of introspection allows you to bring your past experiences to the surface for healing. Every instance in your life where you unintentionally hurt yourself should be brought up as well. Look at those times with a greater sense of compassion, take the lessons from them, and apply them to your life accordingly. I commend you for choosing yourself because it is not easy to swear off those who call you selfish; sometimes it's the people you love the most. BUT that's just the thing… you HAVE to see yourself as a high priority and you have to make sure that they know you're serious about where you stand. You are worthy, and for some reason, I feel like my journey of self-love and self-care can be helpful to someone in their time of need.

    Self-love, self-care, self-confidence, self-compassion, self-worth, self-value, self-respect, self-esteem… You can acquire them all. I have, at one time or another, been lacking in those areas, so I feel that it would be less of me to sit back and watch someone go through life and not speak on how to better adapt. Unfortunately, we are not all taught at an early age how to prioritize ourselves, and that often trickles down throughout the course of our lives. And while that is the case, inherently, it's okay because that's where we learn how to say, "enough is enough." Eventually, we get the gist of why truly loving yourself holds so much weight. As I mentioned a few chapters back, external attainment of "things" will never sustain your happiness, and they will never fill the void that comes with not loving yourself to the best of your ability. This is ultimately about how we see ourselves and what we feel we deserve internally. It's also about how we allow others to treat us, what we allow ourselves to be subjected to, and the firmness/foundation of our mental state. Sometimes we're vulnerable… sometimes we're pressured… sometimes we're just trying to fit in… and sometimes we just don't know what the fuck we're doing. It's as simple as that most of the time. The key is taking action when you notice yourself going astray, and then passing on that knowledge when the opportunity presents itself. That's exactly what I'm trying to do with myself; let my testimony help someone who finds themselves being tested. How we form and develop relationships with ourselves and with others is more important than you think. The interrelation cannot be argued; it can either increase or decrease our social skills, and cause growth or stagnation in our mental, emotional, physical, and spiritual well-being. In the end, love is what matters. When you learn this, my single friend, exude this… become this… shower yourself in this. Hopefully, you will be able to finally wash away everything that keeps you from believing in yourself, your beauty, your strength, and your footsteps towards your purpose, your goals, and your dreams.

Sincerely, Wanna, SBC